MONSTROUS MYTHS

Terrible Tales of Ancient Rome

Clare Hibbert

Gareth Stevens
Publishing

Please visit our website, www.garethstevens.com. For a free color catalog of all our high-quality books, call toll free 1-800-542-2595 or fax 1-877-542-2596.

Library of Congress Cataloging-in-Publication Data

Hibbert, Clare.
Terrible tales of ancient Rome / by Clare Hibbert.
   p. cm. — (Monstrous myth)
Includes index.
ISBN 978-1-4824-0187-5 (pbk.)
ISBN 978-1-4824-0188-2 (6-pack)
ISBN 978-1-4824-0185-1 (library binding)
1. Mythology, Roman — Juvenile literature. I. Hibbert, Clare, 1970- II. Title.
BL803.H53 2014
292.1'3—dc23

First Edition

Published in 2014 by
Gareth Stevens Publishing
111 East 14th Street, Suite 349
New York, NY 10003

Copyright © 2014 Arcturus Publishing

Illustrations: Janos Jantner (Beehive Illustration)
Editor: Joe Harris
Designer: Emma Randall
Cover designer: Emma Randall

All rights reserved. No part of this book may be reproduced in any form without permission from the publisher, except by reviewer.

Printed in the United States of America

CPSIA compliance information: Batch #CW14GS: For further information contact Gareth Stevens, New York, New York at 1-800-542-2595.

CONTENTS

Roman Stories and Legends 4

Aeneas the Adventurer 6

Journey to the Underworld 10

Brotherly Love—Or Not! 14

The Jealous Goddess 18

Life in the Land of the Dead 22

Cupid's Revenge 26

Glossary 30

Further Information 31

Index 32

ROMAN STORIES AND LEGENDS

About 2,000 years ago, Rome was the capital of a powerful empire that stretched across three continents. The Romans believed in many gods, and some of their favorite stories were about these gods. Others told of dashing heroes or big moments in Roman history.

How did the Romans build such an impressive empire? By sending out armies to grab new lands. And how did the Romans come up with so many gods and myths? Well...they grabbed many of those as well!

One of the Romans' own gods was Janus, whose two heads could look into the past and the future.

Almost all of the main Roman gods were based on Greek ones. The Romans changed the names, but their stories were often direct rip-offs. The chief Roman god, Jupiter, for instance, was a dead ringer for the main Greek god, Zeus. Both were sky gods and both brandished thunderbolts. The Romans stole the story of the Greek hero Heracles, too, but renamed him Hercules.

The Romans didn't steal everything. They did have a few myths and gods that were just theirs. One myth told the story of how their empire was founded by twins. And Janus was their two-headed god of doorways, gates, and new beginnings. Janus was said to have once ruled Latium, the region where Rome was later built.

Believe it or not!

The month January, which comes at the beginning of the year, is named after the Roman god Janus.

AENEAS THE ADVENTURER

The hero Aeneas made his first appearance in ancient Greek mythology, but the Romans gave him a real starring role. His mom, they said, was Venus, the glamorous goddess of love, and his dad belonged to the royal family of Troy.

Aeneas was one of Troy's bravest fighters in the war against Greece. After the Greek victory, all that was left of his hometown was burning piles of rubble. Aeneas didn't stick around. His cousin Prince Hector, who'd died in the fighting, appeared to him in a dream. He told Aeneas to leave the city while he still could.

Aeneas set out with a group of Trojan survivors. Their first stop was Thrace, which Aeneas thought would make a good spot for a new home. But when he started clearing the ground, something weird happened. The plant stems spurted blood. Weirder still, the plants spoke! The sinister shrubs had grown from the spears that killed another Trojan prince, Polydorus.

Peculiar possessed plants?! Maybe Thrace wasn't such a good place for a new home after all...

Aeneas decided to try again: he would set up a colony on Crete. But this time, a plague struck, so he took to the seas again. His next stop was the Strophades, a couple of islands inhabited by hideous Harpies. These greedy bird-women took the Trojans by surprise, swooping down to attack when they sat down to eat. One even placed a curse on Aeneas. How rude!

The Harpies were vicious, winged monsters with sharp talons.

Next Aeneas visited King Helenus, another exile from Troy. Helenus warned Aeneas about a wicked whirlpool called Charybdis and told him how to avoid it. Sailing on past the whirlpool, the Trojans reached another island and met a shaggy-haired Greek who begged for a lift. He'd been accidentally left behind by his crew on the island of the Cyclopes, huge one-eyed giants. No wonder the guy didn't want to stay there!

The Trojans were hoping to reach Latium soon, but they hadn't counted on Juno, queen of the gods. She had two reasons to make trouble for them: Aeneas' mom had beaten her in a beauty contest and the contest judge was from Troy. Juno conjured up a storm that carried Aeneas far away to Carthage in north Africa. But it wasn't all bad news...

Dear Mom (and most worshipful goddess),
Greetings from sunny Carthage! I've been enjoying life here. I've fallen in love with Dido, the queen, and could happily stay here forever. What a shame Jupiter had to spoil it by sending the messenger god Mercury to remind me of my duty. I know! I know! I've got to go and found a new city. Blah, blah. I just wish I didn't have to leave Dido. She says she can't live without me.
Your son, Aeneas X

Aeneas did leave Dido and carry on to Latium, because it's never a good idea to ignore the king of the gods. There he founded a city, just as he'd been destined to, and married another royal—a princess called Lavinia.

> Thanks to the advice from King Helenus, Aeneas steered clear of the whirlpool Charybdis. Not all ships were so lucky.

Believe it or not!
The Roman emperor Augustus (who reigned from 27 BCE to 14 CE) claimed that he was descended from Aeneas and Lavinia.

JOURNEY TO THE UNDERWORLD

Aeneas' bravery was really put to the test when he had to venture into Dis, the land of the dead. He was on a quest to meet up with the spirit of his dead father, Anchises. But would it be a one-way trip? No one was supposed to return from the Underworld…

Aeneas' dad was around for most of the journey from Troy to Italy but, sadly, he died on Sicily just before the storm that blew Aeneas to Carthage. Aeneas revisited Sicily on the anniversary of his dad's death. He arranged eight days of sacrifices to the gods in Anchises' honor, followed by a day of sporting competitions, such as boxing.

A boxing match! Now there's a punchy way to show your deep respect for the dead!

That night, Aeneas' father appeared to him and said he must come to the Underworld. First, Aeneas headed to a temple on the Italian coast. He wanted advice from the priestess there, known as the Sibyl. She told Aeneas to find a magical golden bough in the massive forest nearby. It was like looking for a needle in a haystack! Luckily, Venus sent doves to guide Aeneas to the right tree.

When they arrived in Dis, the Sibyl had to sweet-talk the ferryman into carrying them across the river into the Underworld. She said Aeneas was bringing a gift—the golden bough—for Proserpina, the queen of the Underworld.

On the other side of the river, the three-headed hound of hell, Cerberus, was waiting. The clever Sibyl had an answer for him, too—three drugged doggie treats, one for each head. Soon the beast was sleeping like a baby.

Cerberus was Dis' guard dog—but instead of stopping anyone breaking in, he made sure no one ever broke out!

The Underworld was a strange realm, split into different regions. Walking past the Fields of Mourning, Aeneas was horrified to see Dido, the queen he had once loved. He tried to explain that he didn't choose to leave her—the gods made him do it!—but she just turned away. At least she wasn't alone. She had been reunited with her first husband.

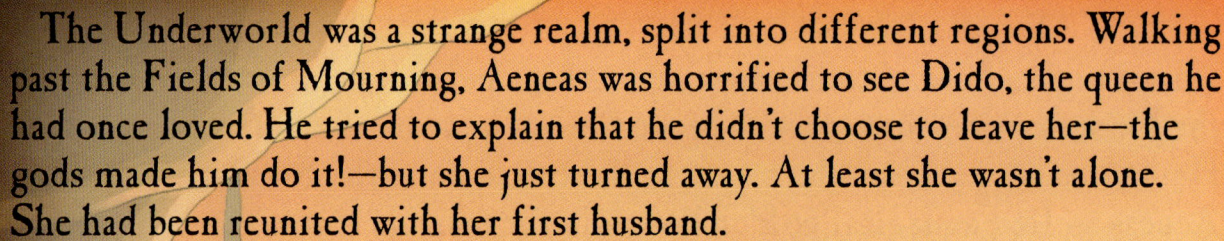

The Furies were demons who made spirits suffer—a job that the horrible hags really enjoyed.

Next was the Field of Warriors. The spirits of Greek soldiers fled at the sight of Aeneas. How strange—he couldn't hurt them now they were dead! Then they came to Tartarus, a prison for evildoers. Aeneas could hear the clanking of chains and the cracking of whips. Demons called Furies flew at the spirits trapped there, tormenting them for eternity.

At the palace of Pluto, king of Dis, Aeneas fixed the enchanted golden bough to the doorway. Thanks to this offering, he and the Sibyl would be allowed to leave the Underworld.

Finally they reached the Elysian Fields, home to the spirits of the good. Aeneas was relieved to see his dad there. Anchises explained that Aeneas' destiny was to father the mighty rulers of Rome. Once he was satisfied that his son understood his duty, Anchises took Aeneas and the Sibyl to a gate to the world of the living. Aeneas had made it back from the land of the dead!

Believe it or not!

In another legend, the Sibyl sold three books of prophecies to Rome's last king, Tarquin the Proud. She would have sold him nine, but he annoyed her by haggling over the price…so she burned six just to spite him!

BROTHERLY LOVE—OR NOT!

Imagine the people of a famous city bragging that its founder was a murderer. That's the story that the ancient Romans used to tell. The legend began with the birth of twin brothers, Romulus and Remus.

The boys' mother, Rhea Silvia, was princess of Alba Longa, a city in Latium, and their father was Mars, the god of war. Rhea Silvia's wicked uncle didn't want any challenges to the throne, so he ordered a servant to kill the babies. Luckily, the servant didn't have the heart to do it. He put the boys in a basket instead and cast it into the River Tiber.

The Tiber carried the babies safely downriver until the basket caught on tree roots near the site of the future city of Rome. A she-wolf who'd just lost her cubs found the boys and mothered them, feeding them her own milk.

> Those twins were really lucky. The she-wolf could easily have 'wolfed' them down as a snack!

Before the twins turned too wild, a kind shepherd found them. He took them home, and he and his wife raised them as their own. The boys grew up having no idea that they were really royalty. They became shepherds like their foster father. Then, one day, Remus got into a fight with some herders from Alba Longa. They carried him off to their king. Romulus gathered a band of followers and marched off to rescue his twin.

Lupa the wolf looked after the boys as if they were her own pups.

In Alba Longa, Romulus freed Remus and the pair discovered who they really were—the city's princes! They killed the wicked great-uncle who'd wrongfully made himself king and gave the throne back to their granddad. Then they set out to found a new city that they could rule.

The brothers agreed roughly where their city should be, but squabbled about which hill to build on. Romulus wanted the Palatine Hill, but Remus preferred the Aventine Hill.

Might Remus come back as a ghost? His brother Romulus feared that restless spirits could haunt the living.

ROMULUS' DIARY – STAY OUT, REMUS!

Dear Diary,

    Remus and I just can't agree on where to build our city. We decided to use an augury to decide the site – it's where you let animals tell you the will of the gods. Remus saw six vultures… but then I saw a dozen! That should've settled it, but oh no! Not good enough for Remus. He's now saying his birds appeared first. Gah! I could kill him sometimes!

Tired of quarrelling, Romulus began to build his city wall. Remus was itching for a fight. First he criticized the wall and then he jumped over it. Romulus saw red. With one blow, he killed his brother and declared he'd do the same to anyone else who tried to cross his city wall uninvited.

With great modesty, Romulus called his city "Rome" after himself! Then he invented a special festival to keep away ghosts, just in case Remus' spirit came back to cause trouble. It involved throwing lots of beans around. It sounds bonkers but it must have done the trick—no ghost interfered with the city becoming amazingly powerful!

Believe it or not!

The Chechen people of Russia have a myth that their heroic founder, Turpalo-Noxchuo, was raised by a wolf mother, too.

THE JEALOUS GODDESS

As the "goddess of love," Venus must have been all warmth and loveliness, right? Wrong! Goddess or not, Venus was less than perfect, and she was really bad at handling jealousy.

Venus was so jealous of the beautiful mortal, Psyche, that she vowed the poor girl would marry a monster!

The story begins in a faraway city, ruled by a king who had three daughters. Psyche, the youngest, was so beautiful that the city folk stopped making offerings to Venus and worshipped their pretty princess instead. Not surprisingly, Venus was furious! She sent her son Cupid to make Psyche fall in love with a beastly being and shame her family. The trouble was that, when Cupid clapped eyes on Psyche, he fell in love with her himself.

Psyche's parents had no idea that a god had a crush on their darling girl. They just thought she needed a husband. So they visited the oracle—a kind of priest—to ask for advice. The oracle told them that Psyche must journey to the top of a mountain, to marry a monster.

Poor Psyche's parents were horrified! But you just couldn't argue with the gods.

Psyche climbed to the top of the mountain, and from there she was carried to her new home by a magical gust of wind. She arrived at a glittering palace filled with sweet music and fabulous food. Her new husband only visited after dark and banned her from looking at him, but he didn't seem very monstrous.

Soon, Psyche began to miss her family and persuaded her husband to let her sisters visit. Bad idea! Envious of Psyche's palace, they just couldn't help stirring up trouble. The sisters said Psyche should sneak a peek at her new husband and, if necessary, kill him.

Of course, when Psyche lit her lamp that night, she found not a grisly monster, but Cupid—the most beautiful man ever! He was also the most angry man ever at that moment, very cross that Psyche had disobeyed him. He flew off, and Psyche had to go looking for him.

Psyche realized her best hope was to impress Venus. The goddess gave her four fiendish tests. First, she made Psyche sort all the mixed-up grains, beans, and seeds in her granary. A colony of ants helped with that job. Next, Venus

Cupid was mad that Psyche disobeyed him, but he couldn't stay annoyed with her forever!

asked for golden wool from the sun god's bad-tempered sheep. This time, a talking river reed came to the rescue. It told Psyche to avoid the sheep and collect wisps of wool caught on bushes instead.

Psyche's third task was to collect black water from the source of two hellish, revolting rivers. There were vile dragons slithering around, and it was no place for a princess! Taking pity on her, the sky god Jupiter sent his eagle to collect the water.

Psyche's last task was to steal some of the beauty of the goddess of the Underworld. Daunted, Psyche climbed a tower, ready to throw herself off, but then the tower spoke! It told her she'd be fine, as long as she took some cakes to bribe the Underworld's guard dog, Cerberus, and some coins to pay for her return journey to the land of the living.

After all her trials, Cupid forgave Psyche. He persuaded his mom to leave them alone so they could live happily ever after.

Believe it or not!

In myths, Cupid carried a bow and arrow that made people fall in love. Today, you can still see him on Valentine's cards!

LIFE IN THE LAND OF THE DEAD

Pluto was the god who ruled over the Underworld. He was very rich thanks to all the gold, silver, and jewels deep underground, but he had no one to share his life with. Venus, the goddess of love, felt rather sorry for him. Never able to keep from meddling, she decided to help Pluto find a wife. She asked her son Cupid to shoot one of his arrows at Pluto so that he'd fall in love.

Sicily's smoking volcano Mount Etna was one place where the Underworld met the mortal realm. The next time Pluto emerged, driving his speedy chariot drawn by four snorting black horses, Cupid was ready and waiting. He took aim and—whoosh!—his arrow hit home. Poor Pluto would fall head over heels for the next girl he saw.

> If his snarling three-headed dog wasn't enough, Pluto could always rely on his two-pronged pitchfork to give people a scare!

"Uh-oh. Cupid's arrows of desire were always causing trouble!"

That girl was beautiful Proserpina, daughter of the sky god Jupiter and the farming goddess Ceres. She was spending the day by one of Sicily's loveliest lakes, hanging out with her nymph friends, picking flowers, and singing sweet songs.

Pluto was smitten, but he didn't have much of a way with girls. In the Underworld, he hadn't needed to know about paying compliments, buying gifts, or taking pretty girls out on dates. Knowing no better, Pluto simply grabbed Proserpina and carried her off. He didn't even seem to notice her angry screams, but probably the one thing the Underworld had taught him was to ignore screaming!

When Proserpina didn't come home that evening, her mom was worried sick. Ceres searched high and low, but her daughter seemed to have disappeared off the face of the earth. Eventually, she found Proserpina's belt and discovered that brutish Pluto had taken her.

Ceres couldn't believe such a terrible thing could happen. As the goddess of crops and farming, she was tremendously powerful. Ceres placed a curse upon the earth saying that no crops would grow until her daughter came back to her.

Proserpina tried not to eat anything while she was in the Underworld, but Pluto tricked her into tasting just a few pomegranate seeds.

Seeing the lands turning to desert and all the people starving, Jupiter sent his messenger, Mercury, to ask Pluto to release Proserpina. The trouble was that if anyone ate or drank in the Underworld, they couldn't leave. Proserpina had eaten some pomegranate seeds. That meant she could only rejoin her mom for part of each year, and must spend the rest, the winter, with Pluto as his queen.

STOP THE PRESS! SPRING ARRIVES

The goddess Proserpina's release from the Underworld today was greeted with a riot of spring flowers. Choking back tears of joy, her mom, Ceres, said she'd made the flowers bloom as a special welcome. Looking ahead to the winter months when Proserpina will have to return to her husband, Ceres confided, "It's meant to be a surprise, but I'm planning a special send-off. I'm going to turn all the leaves red, orange, yellow, and brown – Proserpina's favorite colors."

Believe it or not!

The story of Proserpina being snatched was first told by the ancient Greeks. In their version, she was called Persephone, her husband was Hades, and her mother Demeter. The pomegranate was the same, though!

CUPID'S REVENGE

Apollo was the gorgeous god of the sun, light, and music. He was the god of archery too, while his twin sister Artemis was the goddess of hunting. Handsome, athletic, and brave, Apollo's only real fault was his tendency to boast.

One of Apollo's favorite stories was how he'd shot down a huge and hideous winged serpent.

One day, Apollo saw Cupid with his bow and arrow and began to tease him. Not such a clever idea! First of all, Apollo mocked Cupid's little "weapons" and said he should leave war and fighting to true warriors like himself. Then he went on—rather annoyingly, Cupid thought—to describe how he had battled a huge and horrible serpent. As he yawned along to the god's bragging, a sneaky plan formed in Cupid's mind. "I'll show Apollo just how harmless my bow and arrow are," he thought.

Apollo might have exaggerated a bit about the snake-beast. He claimed its poisonous body was so long it covered acres and acres of land.

Just then the beautiful nymph Daphne was passing. Cupid pierced Apollo through the heart with a golden arrow of desire. Then he let loose a lead arrow in Daphne's direction. The lead arrow did the opposite of the golden one. It made Daphne find the whole idea of marrying anyone absolutely disgusting.

Daphne's dad, the river god Peneus, was not impressed by her attitude. He wanted her to marry and settle down, like any normal nymph. He wanted some cute, adoring grandchildren, too. Daphne insisted point-blank that she wasn't going to marry. Peneus wasn't so sure. He thought she was too beautiful not to.

Apollo certainly agreed with Peneus. Desperate with love by now, he began to chase Daphne. She, of course, ran away. Daphne was just as fast a runner as Apollo, so the pair carried on like this for days.

Eventually Cupid decided to help Apollo with a little boost of speed. Seeing that Apollo was gaining on her, Daphne called out to her father for help. "Please, Dad," she called. "Open the ground to swallow me up! Or, if you can't do that, at least change me into something that Apollo can't marry."

Turning into a tree wouldn't be everyone's idea of a lucky escape, but Daphne really, really, REALLY didn't want to marry Apollo!

The old river god's heart melted when he heard his daughter calling. He didn't want Daphne to spend the rest of her life being chased around by a love-crazed god. The only solution was to transform her. Maybe one of his other children would give him grandkids. Peneus used his divine powers to change her into a laurel tree. Her skin turned to bark, her hair became leaves, her arms became branches, and her feet became roots.

Poor Apollo. Even though Daphne was now a plant, he still had feelings for her. He really couldn't "leaf" her alone! He made the laurel his sacred tree and said he'd look after it forever. He used his powers of eternal youth to make the laurel evergreen. And he also declared that only laurel leaves would be noble enough to make crowns for kings and emperors.

Believe it or not!

Early plant scientists had the story of Apollo and Daphne in mind when they gave the laurel its scientific Latin name: *Daphne.*

GLOSSARY

augury Working out the will of the gods by studying signs, especially signs revealed in the appearance or activity of birds or other animals.

colony (1) A settlement established by people in a new land. (2) An insect community, for example, a colony of ants.

Cyclops A one-eyed giant.

Elysian Fields The blissful part of the Underworld where the spirits of the good live in happy contentment.

empire A group of lands or peoples brought under the rule of a single government or person (emperor).

eternity Forever.

Fury One of the violent winged demons who tortured the spirits of bad people in the Underworld.

granary A place for storing grain.

Latin The language of the ancient Romans.

Latium An ancient territory in Italy in the region where Rome would later rise up.

mortal A being that will die. Ordinary human beings are mortal, whereas gods are immortal (they won't die).

nymph A minor goddess who has power over woodlands, rivers, or other features of nature.

oracle A priest or priestess who can speak on behalf of a god, or the sacred site where they live.

sacrifice Something given as an offering to the gods.

smitten Completely taken over by love.

Tartarus The hateful part of the Underworld where the spirits of evildoers are imprisoned.

Trojan War The 10-year war between the Greeks and the people of Troy that was fought because the Trojan prince Paris had stolen Helen, the king of Sparta's wife.

FURTHER INFORMATION

Further Reading

The Orchard Book of Roman Myths by Geraldine McCaughrean (Orchard Books, 2003)

Roman Myths by Kathy Elgin and Fiona Sansom (Franklin Watts, 2012)

Roman Myths and Legends by Jilly Hunt (Raintree, 2013)

The Two-Faced God by Caroline Lawrence (Orion, 2013)

The Romans: Gods, Emperors, and Dormice by Marcia Williams (Candlewick, 2013)

Rotten Romans by Terry Deary (Scholastic, 2007)

Websites

rome.mrdonn.org/myths.html
A website all about Roman myths aimed specifically at kids.

www.bbc.co.uk/schools/primaryhistory/romans/
The BBC's guide to the world of the ancient Romans.

www.pantheon.org/areas/mythology/europe/roman/
The part of the comprehensive online Encyclopedia Mythica that explores Roman gods and stories.

www.roman-empire.net/children/gods.html
Information on all the main Roman gods and goddesses.

Publisher's note to educators and parents: Our editors have carefully reviewed these websites to ensure that they are suitable for students. Many websites change frequently, however, and we cannot guarantee that a site's future contents will continue to meet our high standards of quality and educational value. Be advised that students should be closely supervised whenever they access the Internet.

INDEX

Aeneas 6–9, 10–13
Anchises 10, 13
Apollo 26–29
Artemis 26
auguries 17
Augustus, Emperor 9

Carthage 8, 10
Cerberus 11, 21, 22
Ceres 23–25
Charybdis 8, 9
Crete 7
Cupid 19–21, 22, 26–28
Cyclopes 8

Daphne 27–29
Dido 8–9, 12
Dis 10, 11–13

Elysian Fields 13

Furies 12, 13

ghosts 16–17
goddesses 6, 8, 11, 18–21, 22, 24–25

gods 4, 5, 8, 10, 13, 14, 19–25, 26–29
Greeks 5, 6, 8, 13, 25

Harpies 7
Hector, Prince 6
Helenus, King 8, 9
Heracles 5
Hercules 5

Janus 4, 5
Juno 8
Jupiter 5, 8, 21, 23, 25

Latium 5, 8, 9, 14
Lavinia 9

Mars 14
Mercury 8, 25
monsters 7, 8, 11, 12, 13, 27

nymphs 23, 27–29

oracles 18, 19

Peneus 27–29
Pluto 13, 22–25
Proserpina 11, 23–25
Psyche 18–21

Remus 14–17
Rhea Silvia 14
Rome 4, 5, 14, 17
Romulus 14–17

Sibyl 11, 13
Sicily 10, 22, 23

Tarquin, King 13
Tartarus 13
Thrace 6
Trojan War 6
Troy 6, 8

Underworld 10–13, 21, 22–25

Venus 6, 11, 18–21, 22

Zeus 5